Contents

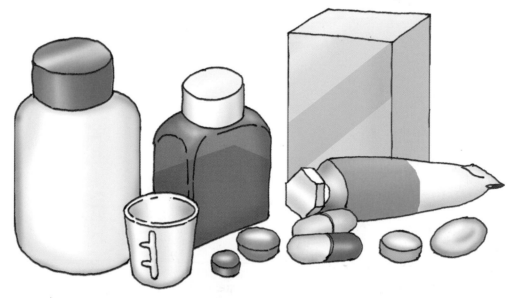

What are drugs?

Drugs are substances that change the way our bodies and minds work. Some drugs help the body to repair itself while others can prevent illness or disease. Drugs from the doctor or chemist can be used to help your body to get back to normal health. However, if they are not used properly, or if they are used for the wrong reasons, they stop being helpful and become dangerous. Some drugs can block the action of natural chemicals in the body.

Medicines help to make you feel better and get your energy back. Although they may make you feel good at first, illegal drugs can make you ill and suffer from bad feelings.

Tobacco, alcohol and illegal drugs, such as ecstasy, can be harmful to your body and mind, and can cause fatal diseases and even death.

Health Matters

Drugs and Your Health

by Jillian Powell

an imprint of Hodder Children's Books

Titles in the series

Drugs and Your Health
Exercise and Your Health
Food and Your Health
Hygiene and Your Health

Editor: Sarah Doughty
Book Editor: Penny McDowell
Design: Sterling Associates
Illustrations: Jan Sterling
Cover design: Tony Fleetwood
Cover photo: Stone (Paul Dance)

First published in Great Britain in 1997 by
Wayland Publishers Ltd

This paperback edition published in 2002 by
Hodder Wayland, an imprint of Hodder Children's Books

Hodder Children's Books
A division of Hodder Headline Limited
338 Euston Road, London NW1 3BH

British Library Cataloguing in Publication Data
Powell, Jillian
Drugs and Your Health – (Health matters)
1. Drugs – Juvenile literature
2. Drug abuse – Juvenile literature
I. Title
613.8

ISBN 0 7502 4180 2

Printed in Hong Kong

Picture acknowledgements
Allsport 21(top); Format 23 (top right); Sally & Richard Greenhill
Photo Library 14; The Hutchison Library 28; Popperfoto 22 (bottom
left); Science Photo Library 8 (both), 23 (centre left & right); South
American Pictures 12; Tony Stone 4, 6, 7, 11, 15, 22 (right), 24,
26; Topham 13; Wayland Picture Library 9; Zefa Picture Library
10, 16, 18, 20, 21 (bottom), 23 (top left).

Right: There are hundreds of different types of drugs. They come as tablets, capsules, liquids or creams and some can be inhaled or injected.

Some drugs are more powerful than others. The effect that a drug has on your body depends on your age, size and health.

Right: Tea, coffee and cola drinks may all contain the drug caffeine. Caffeine is an addictive drug. If you drink eight cups of coffee a day (500–600 mg of caffeine) your body will get used to caffeine. When you stop drinking it, you may have headaches and feel grumpy and unwell.

Drugs that make you better

Drugs that make illness or pain better are called medicines. They include painkillers, cough and cold medicines, diarrhoea and stomach settlers, and antihistamines for allergies such as hayfever. Antibiotics are drugs that fight infections by killing bacteria in the body.

Some medicines can be bought from chemists or in shops and supermarkets. Others have to be prescribed by a doctor.

The doctor works out which drug and how much the patient needs, and checks the details on a computer. The patient then takes the prescription to a chemist to get the drugs.

Right: The body has its own immune system for fighting germs and illnesses. Viruses such as colds and some stomach upsets can often be cured simply by resting and drinking lots of liquids.

Left: There is no cure for colds and flu but there are medicines which can help you to feel more comfortable. Find out from a pharmacist which drugs they contain and how they work.

Living longer

Modern medicines mean that people can expect to live twice as long as they used to hundreds of years ago. As more people live on into their eighties, they may suffer from diseases such as arthritis or heart disease. Drugs can help them to stay alive and to live more comfortably.

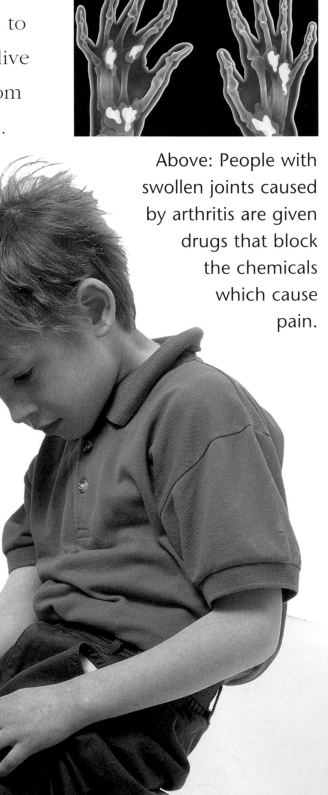

Above: People with swollen joints caused by arthritis are given drugs that block the chemicals which cause pain.

People with high blood pressure are given drugs that block a chemical which makes the blood vessels tighter and so the blood can flow more easily.

Some people need to take drugs all their lives to help them live a normal life. People with diabetes don't have enough of a chemical called insulin which the body needs to break down and use as sugar. They have to inject themselves every day with insulin which is made by scientists in a laboratory.

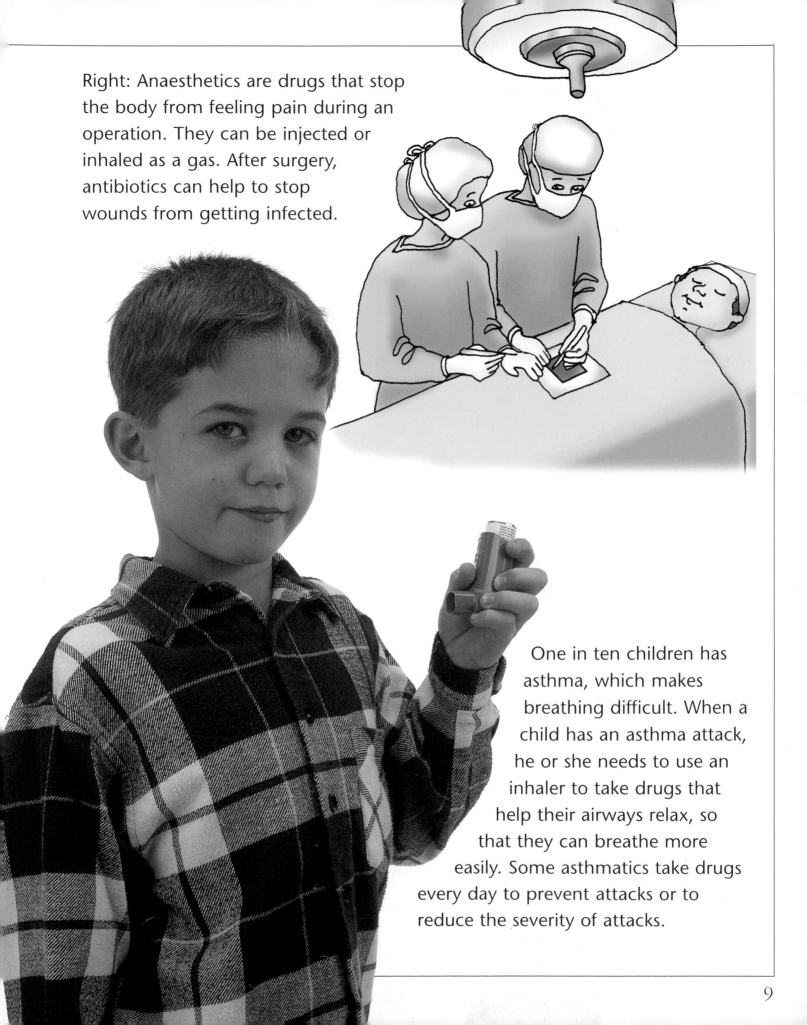

Right: Anaesthetics are drugs that stop the body from feeling pain during an operation. They can be injected or inhaled as a gas. After surgery, antibiotics can help to stop wounds from getting infected.

One in ten children has asthma, which makes breathing difficult. When a child has an asthma attack, he or she needs to use an inhaler to take drugs that help their airways relax, so that they can breathe more easily. Some asthmatics take drugs every day to prevent attacks or to reduce the severity of attacks.

How drugs are made

Drugs are made in laboratories from chemicals that are either man-made or taken from plants or animals. It can take years to find and test a new drug. Scientists look for drugs that will match natural chemicals in the body.

They start by designing chemical models on a computer screen, then make up the drugs in the laboratory and begin tests. Tests may be carried out on dead animal flesh, then on live laboratory animals such as mice or rats.

Scientists are always looking for new drugs to cure diseases such as cancer, multiple sclerosis and HIV.

Some people feel that animals should not be used to test drugs for humans. Many scientists feel that it is better to test a drug that may be dangerous on animals before it is given to humans.

If these tests are successful, the drug is given to groups of human volunteers, to make sure that it is safe to be given to patients.

Right: Plants have been used as medicine for thousands of years. Many modern drugs contain plant extracts. Digitalis, from foxglove leaves, is used in drugs for heart disease. Opium from poppies is used to make painkillers such as morphine.

Find out about as many medicines and drugs that come from plants as you can. Visit a health shop and look in magazines for advertisements for drugs which use plant extracts.

Drugs in the past

People have been using drugs for thousands of years, for medicine or relaxation, or during religious ceremonies and celebrations.

The peoples of the Andes in South America chewed coca leaves, which contain cocaine, to boost their energy, and opium and cannabis were widely used in Asia to kill pain and bring relaxation. Tobacco was smoked by Amerindian tribes and the Aztecs of Mexico used magic mushrooms, which made them feel strange and see things that weren't actually there, during their religious ceremonies.

A woman sells coca leaves to a Quecha Indian at a market in the highlands of Peru. When the dried leaves are chewed, it makes people feel excited and boosts their energy.

Right: In the 1920s, alcohol was banned in the United States by a law called Prohibition. This led to the illegal making and smuggling of alcohol until the law ended in 1933.

Left: Some pilots during the Second World War took amphetamines (purple hearts) to keep them awake.

Right: In the 1950s and 60s, cannabis and LSD (acid) were popular drugs for young people involved in the Flower Power movement.

How drugs work

Drugs come in many forms. Some can be injected into the blood or inhaled so that they start to work immediately. Others need to work more slowly and gradually. Tiny particles are coated in capsules which release them in stages.

Our body cells have special pieces called receptors which receive the chemicals. They have a particular shape and when matching chemicals reach them, they join together in the same way as jigsaw pieces. Drugs can copy natural chemicals in the body or stop them from working.

It is important to measure the right amount of medicine into the measuring spoon.

Syringes work like bicycle pumps, using air pressure to pump medicine down the fine metal tube of the needle into the bloodstream.

pressure

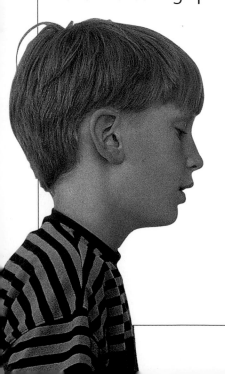

Blood carries drugs to the body cells which need them.

Some drugs are broken down in the liver and only a small amount gets into the blood.

Some drugs have to be injected because stomach juices would destroy them.

Drugs which are not needed pass through the kidneys and out of the body as urine.

Body size affects how a drug works.

Drugs taken by mouth begin to break down in the stomach. Food helps some drugs to work more quickly.

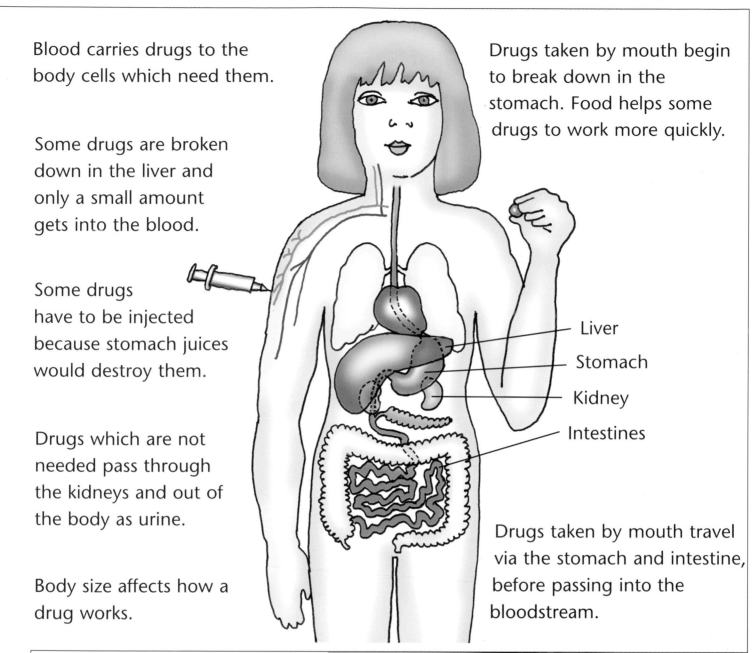

Liver

Stomach

Kidney

Intestines

Drugs taken by mouth travel via the stomach and intestine, before passing into the bloodstream.

Some medicines are made specially for children. Find out about as many children's medicines as you can. In what ways are they different from adults' medicines?

Safety and drugs

All drugs can be harmful if they are not used properly. Labels carry important safety information. They give the correct dosage, measured in milligrams (mgs) for tablets and millilitres (mls) for liquids. They tell the patient how often to take the drug, and whether to take it before, with or after food.

Some drugs must not be taken with alcohol or certain foods, such as milk which can stop antibiotics from working properly. Labels warn of side-effects such as feeling sleepy or that the patient should not use machinery while they are taking the drug.

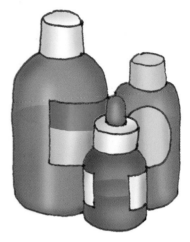

Above: Drugs must be stored in a cool, dark place because light and heat can spoil them. Dark blue or brown glass or plastic keep out sunlight. Some medicines have a 'use by' date.

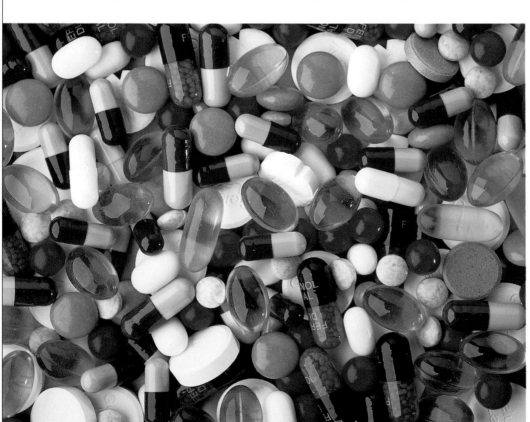

Left: Colourful tablets and capsules can look like sweets to small children. They should be kept out of reach in a medicine cupboard. Special caps stop children from being able to open bottles and jars.

It is important never to take someone else's medicine, even if you think you have the same illness. It could be dangerous and is against the law.

Imagine that you have to put together the contents of a new medicine and first-aid cupboard for your school. What would you include and why? What safety measures would you take to keep drugs safe?

Drinking and smoking

In many countries, tobacco and alcohol are the most commonly used legal drugs. People use them to feel more lively or relaxed, but both are addictive drugs which can harm the body. More people die from heart and lung diseases because of the nicotine in tobacco smoke than from any other drug.

Right: If a woman is pregnant, alcohol or tobacco can harm or even kill her unborn baby.

Below: Passive smoking means breathing in other people's smoke. Fifteen per cent is breathed in by the smoker while the rest goes into the air around.

Many adults and teenagers drink alcohol. In fact, drinking a small amount of alcohol can be good for people. Although there are safe amounts of alcohol that can be drunk, too much of it can kill people by damaging their livers. Alcohol abuse is also the cause of many road accidents and violent crimes.

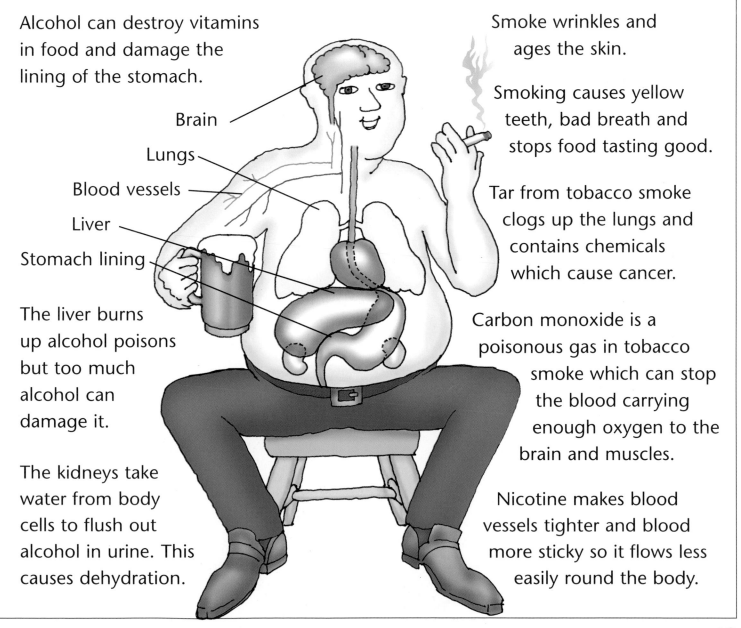

Alcohol can destroy vitamins in food and damage the lining of the stomach.

Brain

Lungs

Blood vessels

Liver

Stomach lining

The liver burns up alcohol poisons but too much alcohol can damage it.

The kidneys take water from body cells to flush out alcohol in urine. This causes dehydration.

Smoke wrinkles and ages the skin.

Smoking causes yellow teeth, bad breath and stops food tasting good.

Tar from tobacco smoke clogs up the lungs and contains chemicals which cause cancer.

Carbon monoxide is a poisonous gas in tobacco smoke which can stop the blood carrying enough oxygen to the brain and muscles.

Nicotine makes blood vessels tighter and blood more sticky so it flows less easily round the body.

Drugs in Sport

Some sportspeople use drugs to build muscle, give them energy, or calm their nerves and hide pain. Some of the drugs they take can be used legally as medicine but are banned from sports. Others are illegal drugs.

When drugs are taken, they pass into the blood then out of the body as urine. Sports authorities take urine samples from sportspeople before and after major sports events. If drugs are found in their urine, they may be banned from the sport for months, years or sometimes forever.

Some sportspeople take drugs to try and help them win. Others believe taking drugs is cheating and campaign against drug use in sport.

Below: Anabolic steroids act like male hormones and build muscle. They are taken as tablets or injected into the muscles. They are legal as medicine but banned from sports and they can have dangerous side-effects such as heart disease, liver cancer and mood changes.

Above: Some athletes will take illegal drugs such as cocaine and amphetamines to make them more energetic and competitive. They are addictive drugs and have side-effects including high blood pressure and heart rate.

Below: Beta-blockers are used to slow down the heart rate and calm nerves. Doctors can prescribe them legally but they can cause heart and breathing problems if misused.

Left: Sometimes, sports players need to take drugs for injuries. Painkillers may let a player continue even after injury.

Illegal drugs

Drugs which some people use illegally are the kind that go to the brain to make strange feelings happen. They can make people feel excited and happy, or relaxed and sleepy, or dizzy and strange. Some illegal drugs can make people see things which are not actually there.

Below: Nine illegal drugs – (left to right): heroin, ecstacy, cannabis leaves (top row), magic mushroom, acid (LSD), cannabis resin (centre row), cocaine, crack cocaine and speed (bottom row).

They can also make you feel bad about yourself and harm your body and mind. Many people who use them start to need more as they spend more time feeling bad and less time feeling good.

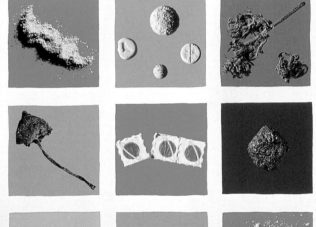

Some people take ecstasy (E) in clubs to give them more energy. It can cause overheating called heatstroke and some people have even died from taking it.

Above: Cocaine is injected or sniffed. A similar drug called crack is smoked or sniffed. They speed up heart rate and give energy, but they are addictive and can cause panic and terrible anxiety.

Amphetamines boost energy but can cause panic, eating and sleeping problems, and may damage blood vessels.

Right: LSD (acid) is a hallucinogenic drug which makes people feel strange and see odd pictures in their heads. They can cause fear, panic and strange behaviour.

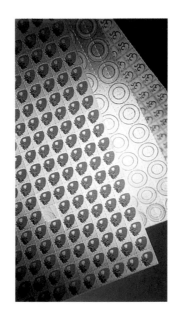

Left: Smoking cannabis makes people feel relaxed, but it can cause lung cancer and make people think less clearly. It has been linked with anxiety and sad feelings.

Solvents are everyday products which give off a strong gas or fumes, such as glue, aerosol sprays, lighter fuel and nail varnish. Some people sniff or spray them into their mouths to feel excited or strange. They contain powerful chemicals which harm your body and could kill you.

Addictive drugs

Addiction is when the mind and body start to need a drug. Addictive drugs include alcohol, nicotine, tranquillizers, cocaine and heroin. They cause chemical changes in the body which make it need more of the drug.

Often, drug addicts can't think of anything except getting more drugs. For a while, the drug makes them feel better, but when they stop using it, they get sick with pain and anxiety. Many crimes, such as stealing and shoplifting, are carried out by some drug addicts who take drugs such as cocaine and heroin, because they are desperate to get more money to buy these expensive drugs.

Babies whose mothers are drug addicts may be born addicted to the same drugs.

The effects of taking ecstacy on the body.

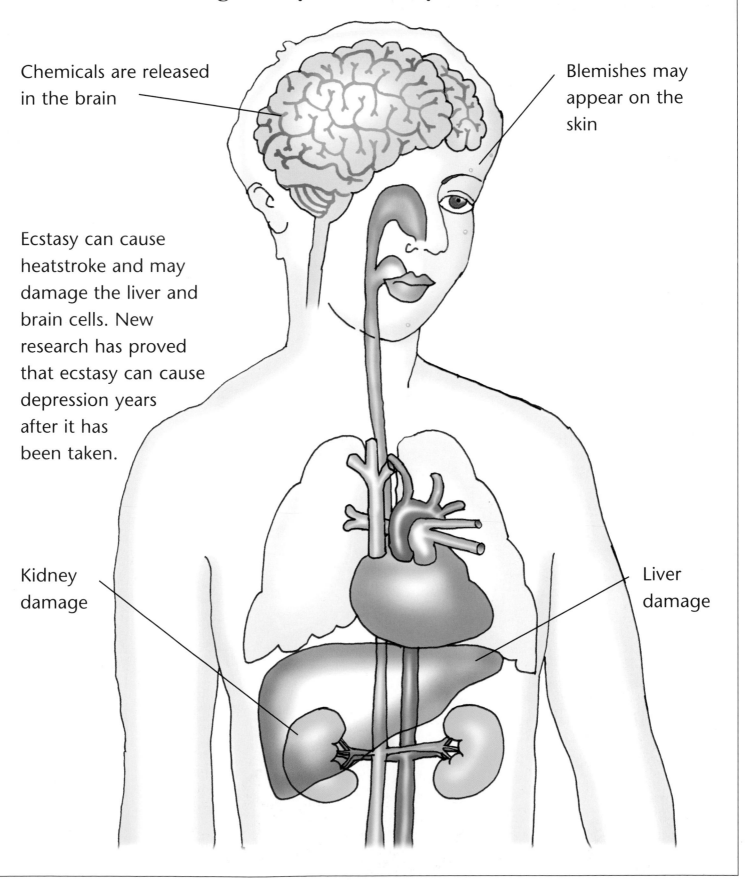

Chemicals are released in the brain

Blemishes may appear on the skin

Ecstasy can cause heatstroke and may damage the liver and brain cells. New research has proved that ecstasy can cause depression years after it has been taken.

Kidney damage

Liver damage

Problems with drugs

Illegal drugs are a growing problem. Drug dealers make a lot of money by selling them and often sell drugs so that they can afford drugs for themselves. People are constantly getting sick and dying from taking illegal drugs. Sometimes, dealers are caught and sent to prison. Drugs coming into a country are sometimes found by the police before they reach the dealers.

A customs officer takes a sniffer dog on to an aeroplane to check that there are no drugs hidden there.

Most countries have laws about drugs. In Britain, the United States and Australia, possessing or selling drugs such as cocaine or heroin is illegal. It is also against the law to take any legal medicines that have been prescribed for somebody else.

In some Muslim countries, alcohol is illegal. Customs officers at ports and airports try to stop people bringing illegal drugs into their country. They use specially trained sniffer dogs to help them to find hidden packets of drugs.

Illegal drugs do not have safety checks as legal drugs do. They may be mixed with flour, talcum powder, chalk dust or even poisonous substances. Sometimes tablets sold as drugs have been found to be other substances such as dog worming pills.

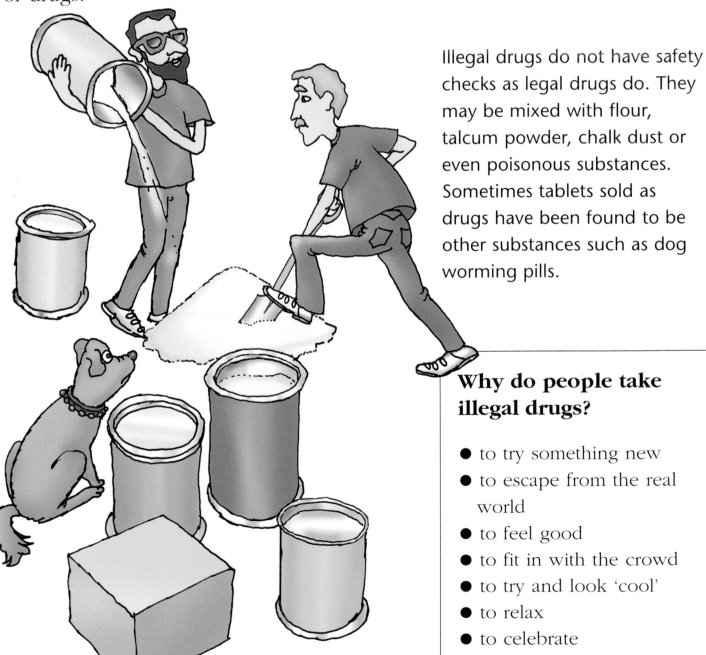

Why do people take illegal drugs?

- to try something new
- to escape from the real world
- to feel good
- to fit in with the crowd
- to try and look 'cool'
- to relax
- to celebrate

The good and the bad

It is important to remember that drugs prescribed or bought from a chemist are there to make you feel better. These drugs are carefully tested in laboratories before they are given to people. If it were not for the many medicines available, there would be more illnesses that could not be cured. It would also mean that returning to full health after an illness would take much longer.

But, illegal drugs can make you sick and harm your body and mind. Any good feelings they give don't usually last for long. There are lots of other ways to feel good and look after your body.

Swimming and playing with your friends not only makes you feel good, it is also good exercise and helps to keep your body healthy.

Dancing, swimming and running can make you feel good and happy. This is because your body makes natural chemicals called endorphins when you exercise. They go to your brain and make you feel good.

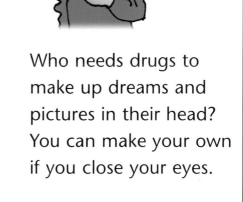

Rollercoasters, cartwheels and somersaults can make you feel strange and dizzy.

Who needs drugs to make up dreams and pictures in their head? You can make your own if you close your eyes.

If someone tries to get you to taste or sniff a strange substance, you need to decide what is right and safe for you. Saying 'no' may be harder than saying 'yes', but learning to stand up for yourself is part of growing up.

Glossary

Addictive Something that you get used to and come to need.

Allergies When the body reacts badly to something.

Amphetamines Man-made chemicals that speed up heart rate and breathing and make you feel excited.

Anaesthetics Substances given to patients so that they feel no pain.

Antihistamines Substances that reverse the effects of allergies.

Bacteria Tiny living things. Some are helpful but others can cause illness.

Caffeine A drug that speeds up your heart rate found in tea leaves and coffee beans.

Dehydration Extreme lack of fluid in the body.

Dosage The amount of medicine to be taken each time.

Hallucinogenic Something which causes strange pictures in the head.

HIV Human Immunodeficiency Virus – one of two viruses that cause AIDS.

Hormones Chemicals that are made in the body.

Immune system The body's own way of protecting itself from illness.

Intestine The long tube that runs from the stomach to the anus.

Multiple sclerosis An illness that causes paralysis and speech defects that becomes gradually worse and has no cure.

Pharmacist The person at the chemist who measures out medicine from the doctor's prescription.

Prohibition A law that stops people from making or selling alcohol.

Tranquillizers Drugs that are used to calm people down; they are often used illegally.

Vaccines A weak form of disease injected to give protection against it.

Books to read

Drugs and Medicine Jenny Bryan (Wayland, 1992)

The Don't Spoil Your Body Book Claire Rayner (Bodley Head, 1989)

What do You Know About Drugs? Pete Sanders and Steve Myers
(Aladdin, 1995)

Drugs and Solvents: A Young Person's Guide (Department of Health)

The Good Health Guide To Drugs (Channel 4 Schools, 1994)

For information about drugs

National Drugs Helpline
Freephone: 0800 776600

Institute for the Study of Drug Dependence
32 Loman Street
London
SE1 OEE

Index